HaunchHigh

Anastasia Stelse

FIRST EDITION, September 2025
ISBN 978-1-953136-90-9 HARDBACK
ISBN 978-1-965784-02-0 PAPERBACK

Cover Graphic Design & Book Typography by Kurt Lovelace.
Cover by PIERIAN SPRINGS PRESS.
Cover type *Bauhaus Dessau* **Alfarn** by Céline Hurka,
Elia Preuss, Flavia Zimbardi,
Hidetaka Yamasaki, and Luca Pellegrini.
Author name, blurbs, footers in **Jenson** by Robert Slimbach.
Back cover description in **Gill Sans Nova**.
Titles and body text set in **Baskerville**.
Flourishes set in Emigre Foundry **Dalliance** by Frank Heine.
Emigre Foundry **ZeitGuys** by Bob Aufuldish, Eric Donelan.
Typefaces licensed Adobe, Linotype, Emigre, & URW GmbH.

PSPRESS.PUB
PIERIAN SPRINGS PRESS, INC
30 N GOULD ST, STE 25398
SHERIDAN, WYOMING 82801-6317

Were I of greater birth I would not be here,
but there is no other place for the common, so I drink
sick-sweet honey from the pool of Lethe,
forget who I was,

          who I am.

from ΑΘΗΝΑΙΣ
PAGE 4, LINES 26-30

 CONTENTS

I

II

III

HaunchHigh

I

The House On Big Spring Drive

The corn, not yet knee-high, will line the left-hand ditch,
coming north. Overgrown with cattails ripening
and red osier dogwood reaching for the barbed wire,
a pasture where cows no longer roam (he's dead).

Pause awhile at the thin, reedy tree where the ditch
drops low and bellows out. Here in the shallows, we
caught bullfrogs, tadpoles, in gallon ice cream buckets—
barefoot and grass-bitten—carried them down that road,

crumbling then, now tarred sticky black I'm told, and knee-
deep in grasses, follow the creeping grape-like vine
to the point where it twists up the elm. Such choking
intricacy. Rip it down—see the gravel drive,

feel the rocks bite the soles of your feet like secrets
heavy kept. Left, the hand-stacked stones of the fountain,
drenched in moss, pond edges strangled by wildflowers.
Straight, the house. Go back ten years. Walk in. Know me then.

Dilemma

The ball-joint of his thumb hidden metal
and the index a snip shorter than
the other—This is what I think of
holding Grampa's severed hand in my

post-stress, over-coffeed hallucination.
Arthritis and a deli slicer—accidents
of another life. The bird in his hand
unmoving, he snaps the neck

back in place and like a white lounge
chair bordering Pleasant Lake,
the bird completes the landscape
as his hands burst into body. *How*

did you learn to fix them?—he's done
it all my life. *You can't save everyone*—
he glances at the knick-knack shelf where
a hummingbird bares its ruby throat.

Organizing The Junk Drawer

Gramma hands me special shears
      for cutting flowers, says she no

          longer any need for blooms
      displayed on her mantle, slender

stalks embalmed briefly with
      vinegar, sugar, water.

ΑΘΗΝΑΙΣ

A puff of winter wind, as psyche, I tremble
from the flesh, tumbling over parched lips
to rest a while in the house of my father
while the women do their work to send me forth—
Prothesis:
        Body bathed in sweet waters, laid for loves to see.
Ekphora:
        Pink painted dawn barely peaks as I am led
past the limits of Athens.

I journey down,
deeper than the ocean floors
Nikethos and I scoured for shells
against our fathers' wills.
Dropping down nine nights
to Tartarus, never again to climb
the mountains in search of the gods,
bearing iridescent necklaces as offerings
for the blessing his father would not give.

Hades opens with a groan, drops
me on the silty shore. Mists creep
from the river, circling round the spires of the far wall
to three dog mouths grinning at the gate.
An obolus pressed to rough hands
and I am rowed forth, rocking
love songs silent on my lips.

Were I of greater birth I would not be here,
but there is no other place for the common, so I drink
sick-sweet honey from the pool of Lethe,
forget who I was,
                    who I am.

A Handbook For Personal Archaeology

Trowel

N.—any of the spade-like tools carried
on the body of an archaeologist with
the explicit intention of moving dirt
in 2-centimeter passes. V.—to trowel,
troweling. The act of bending over
soil, back hunched, spine nearly breaking
skin in a furious attempt to retrieve
knowledge of the lost ones,
or even the lost ones themselves.

BCE

Before Common Era. Nonreligious term
for AD (*Anno Domini*). Way of cataloguing

time. Before, there were other ways. After
will be other ways. The past is never still.

Provenance

N.—[1]the exact—*exact*—
location in which an artifact
was discovered. Looting

destroys provenance.
Without provenance we lose

most of what could be
learned from an artifact.
[2]Home.

Artifact

N.—anything left behind by a culture
or people. What archaeologists
use to study the past. Includes pieces
of tools, refuse, knuckle bones buried or
used in games. Hair, the dagger in the chest,
memories—collective or otherwise.
Fragments, lives. Impossible. Fully.

Farm Work, 1965

His father hands him a shovel
and nods out the barn door.
One of the barn cats wobbles

in the yard, fur missing
from the scruff of her neck
which she stops to try to lick.

Loosening fur fluffs off, catches
the wind.
—*Distemper*—his father says, pokes

a German finger in the boy's back,
nudging him into the day's
impossible harshness.

His father doesn't lecture,
doesn't need to—the boy knows.

The cat stumble-weaves
through his legs and the boy steadies
himself, steps back, shovel raised—

13th September 1811

2 large, 1 small
Mr. Hill had heard talk of the small—
assured no disease, street accident.
In good enough condition. Fetched
£5.10s. Took large to St. Pancras.
Wary after dogs time before. Sent
party on scout. Clear night.

A Short History Of Embalmment

Dr. Thomas Holmes, 1863

Colleagues of Our Esteemed Art—
It is the body we seek to keep
a little longer on the field of battle—
bodies blown and bayonetted.
We sift through internal sullage
for captains, generals—those
whose families will pay for the treatment
and the train trip back home.
Even the faintest whiff of rot
will send a corpse rail side.
A pity, but also fact. And now,
preventable. I've seen to that.
An old problem—of scientists,
of our modern medical schools—
this swift decay, the downward
sway of cadavers, flesh falling
off bone like boiled chickens.
Da Vinci himself,
played the game of preservation,
pricked and drained wrists and veins.
1616—Dr. William Harvey discovers
what Da Vinci suspected—tangled
weave of arteries, veins, capillaries
connected, circulating our blood.
It was all a matter of time.
Trials and errors, cadavers
and quicksilver, embalmers
with bleeding gums and the heavy breath
of death. Killing themselves to save

the dead from the inevitable—no,
not even the dead, the empty
receptacles of once humans.
And the public didn't take kindly
to this new practice.
Called it *unnatural*—but
I'm getting ahead of myself—
in France, a shift to alcohol but the alcohol,
it wasn't quite right. The paled body
pale a little longer. A little longer
did not melt. So to France I went
and arsenic! An experiment
in phrenology and vigorous study
of dry-faced Egyptian mummies—
coarse, hairless, exceptionally fragile—
tanned with mixtures of saline and sap…
I could forgo the deadly chemicals.
Concocted an arterial replacement fluid:
arsenic, zinc, creosote, turpentine—
one day they'll call me
the father of modern embalming.
Now we stand on a great battlefield
of this our Civil War, and I have men
checking the pockets
of our brave deceased,
searching for my card and a signed statement—
I'll get them home. They will be like themselves.

Caipirinha

July, I sit with lightning bugs and mosquitoes
on a warm northern porch
watching the sky fade into my glass
and the stars peek out over the fields.

On the Fourth you can see fireworks
from three small towns just by turning
in a circle—that's how nowhere I am.
I am no one's someone drinking cachaça

mixed with sugar crushed in lime,
drinking away the memories of Paris,
you, and distance. With little click-ticks
bugs bounce off the lanterns.

I was wrong—I can't live
with the bullfrogs' chorus bleating
in my ears, knowing you've left me
for home, drunk with fear.

Science For The Dead

In the lower Engadine Valley,
twenty-eight hundred years ago,
Swiss men farmed. Evidence
litters the landscape. In the hut,
four feet beneath the packed dirt floor
baby bones awaken at archaeologists'
hands. They crate you: swaddle
you in plastic, cotton and packing peanuts,
deliver you from the softly swaying van
to the moonshine steel of my lab.
First formalities: x-ray the bundle,
scan your 3-D form into computers,
send the tiny shroud to the pollen people.
Laid out soft bones against hard steel
the braille holes in your skull read rickets.
Your jaw twists downward at the chin
the whole bone pocked and pitted,
too weak to hold itself up. Your ribs flare
like the ends of tiny flutes, playing
a tale of malnutrition,
poor mineralization, vitamin D deficiency.
A winter baby, my guess,
swaddled to death. Wrapped head
to toe for warmth against the icy
valley air, starved for sunlight
by new parents. They would not have known.
The pollen people say you were buried
early spring, pollen related to our bright
blue alpine asters embedded in the linen
you were wrapped in.

Sustenance

To the bee
the vast aqua marine
of my dress
is nothing less
than a blue pool
of nectar, waiting
to be tapped
and lapped, licked
and carried,
in the last warmth
of days. Summer
greenly fades.
To the bee, these
legs are browning wheat,
signs of seasons
shifting late,
cues
to scream, reasons
to hibernate.

Dirt

Like a dandelion or a Cabbage
Patch Kid, covered in mud's
muck, I breathed sun
and lengthened faster
than my friends.

Born in winter, as fluffs
of white bathed
sidewalks—dirt frozen,
I would not come to know it
for some months.

I will wrap myself in it,
smooth the soft clay
over aching joints,
immerse myself, forget breathing,
return to where I'm from.

29ᵗʰ September 1811

Found watch at St. Pancras, party
to Newington. 1 large. Jack procures.
Hattie does not want him near
the children. Large to Mr. Rhine. £6.20s.

The Archaeologist In Childhood

I once found a cracked Mickey spoon, not the whole thing, just
the dirt-caked plastic handle where the metal once attached.

That was the beginning of digging. Grade school curiosity
        pockmarked
the backyard; a desire to find something—anything—of life
        here before.

Instead I excavated the spoon from the crabgrass that was once
        our garden.
My short history cycled back—the matching fork still

in the kitchen drawer even though we three kids
were too old for it, even back then. It's still there now,

and I am hundreds of miles gone, but I know back home,
        untouched,
in a shoebox in my room lays the spoon, flecked with dirt,
        beside a chunk

of beaver-bit wood, a gnawed on T-bone, the scavenged
        body of a bird,
and a hermit crab—claws clenched in ocean longing—artifacts

of lives stumbled across, adopted—the dead
preserved the only way I knew then.

The Phrenologist To His Apprentice

You tremor with morality, boy.
It is more immoral to waste
what could be studied, like the Dutch
Fiddler here. Cranioklepty, they may

call it—but what point is there in letting
the dead rest in peace? Much better
rest in pieces! For science's sake,
of course. It is best to get them fresh,

strip flesh yourself—it is the only way
to ensure identity. How, you ask?
Make friends with local undertakers,
first to hear who's gone. Be prepared

to pay and well—the greater the name,
the greater specimen of study, hilled
modules marked most precisely
in their wisdom—we cannot let those fall

into the hands of lesser men. Take hold
of the craniometer—smooth caliper
of our craft—notice Aggression's
Desert of Bone. You'd suspect

a mountain with 34 confessed murders
residing there; instead, feel the Peak
of Wonder, the crest at the edges. Bumps
of Benevolence even. It is not always

obvious—that's the beauty of it.
A combative nature did not send
our elderly gent to murder—it was wonder,
that primitive joy at the sight of blood.

November, 1957

Sun shifts through oaks as women talk,
their eyes far off over the dry husked farmlands.
Grace lists what she's learned so far of marriage,
so far of motherhood, her tricks for putting a baby to sleep.

Too soon her friend must leave, must head back to the city.
The car door's crash startles sparrows from the trees and Grace,
poised to wave, glances to her child. Eyes dart—

bushes   tree   friend, braking suddenly.
Headlines of the last month firefly—

> Russians Launch Dog into Space,

> World's Longest Suspension

> Bridge Opens in Mackinac Straits,

> New Witnesses in Levelland UFO Sightings—

Child Run Over—

Not far off, her daughter, red ball abandoned,
fuzzy blonde head peeking up through hydrangeas
at field ants traversing dead blooms.

Out Of Childhood

June 1999

The children are knee deep in the ditch again,
shaded by red osier dogwood and stray elms.
Cattail stalks make their slow climb to maturation
as do the tadpoles the children stalk, thrusting
miniature fists in murky water, pulling up palms
full of mud full of critters. Ashlee squeals.
A black tail wiggles along her life lines.
The others swarm, giggle. This tadpole doesn't have a head,
this tadpole isn't a tadpole. "Leech!" They scream,
laugh as their cousin throws the blood worm at them.
She clambers out of the ditch into biting grasses, huffing
her way barefoot down the gravel road.

The Snapper

Up from the ditch—
cattails higher than July corn—
a twenty-pound snapper stalled
near the road. She sits, claws
dug deep in dirt, shell disguised
under algae thick as fleece.
Maria and I watch,
gathering sticks for our grandparents.

The cat paws over, curious.
His hiss and her hiss mingle
with the slow trudge
of the shallow water ditch
and the wind's shudder
through corn stalks.

A truck blows by, churning gravel.
Scaly-eyed, our snapper thrashes
her head, tears at the air—
invader to our realm.

This displaced ancient
could still tear a finger off—
rip through flesh,
sever tendons.
She clamps our stick, starved
for a territorial violence flashed
between our child-eyes,
the stick's shredding bark rough
against our palms. Her curved talons
tear wiry crabgrass,
unearthing pockets of dirt

—digging—

The clench of her Jurassic jaw tightens
as we tow her drying body to the ditch
guiding her to murky water's edge instead.
We wait for her to get her bearings,
belly down and clamber in,
dissolve into mud.

3rd October 1811

Slow season. 1 small. Hunger-
bitten and fevered. Poor wretch.
Jack wanted to take it regardless
but there's no money in that.

Prophecy

The tongue-tip words I don't let fall will be forgotten.
The loved one's words I won't recall will be forgotten.

A snap in the chest—the wasp nest lodged there crashes down.
My hurried accent, his slow drawl, will be forgotten.

I will die. My brother's son will receive the inheritance.
The antique dolls and Grandmother's shawl will be forgotten.

Headline—Darkness Dethrones Sun As Universal God.
These silent shadows on the wall will be forgotten.

Silence, silence will wear your writings as a dress.
The secrets beneath the words you scrawl—we'll be forgotten.

Keeping On

East of Little Burg, the rivers open
into a lacework of trees and cabined lakes.
Dawn draws me from bed at 4 AM.
I hitch canoe after canoe onto my truck.

This early, tourists close their ears to the call
of the northern saw-whet owl. Near
the cabins, fish scaling sheds—catchalls
for waste. The tourists, never trained by fear,
do not offer guts to placate the owl's shrieking.

A wolf stalks deer trails at night.
But they are rare, disappearing like snow, leaking
through bone rivers. Fur pure white
and fading. The ground below us hollowed.
My father died. I mixed his ashes with river. Swallowed.

Curveball, 1963

Sparrows whir in the barn rafters,
safe from cats creeping
along the hayloft beams.
The chickens are gone—heads
cocked off, feathers
strewn, pimply-fleshed in freezers.
The boys shut the windows, lock
double paneled red paint peeling doors
while autumn light, golden as corn husks
drips through the glass panes.
A sparrow tries to leave, can't, flails around
exciting others. The cats prowl, tails low.
The boys grin, take position
at opposite ends of the barn,
baseball bats in hand. The cousin cocks
his hat, shoulders up to the plate and waits
for the curveball bird hurdling
towards the exit. It hooks
and he takes the swing. The other boy
steadies and responds with a *crack*.
The feathers fly,
barn cats backflipping as birds rain
in broken fluffs. It's in this way
they learn to hit the curveballs
they'll one day teach their sons.
It's in this way they ready the barn
for spring, the chicks they'll raise
then close their eyes
when the fathers take them away.

Virgin—BCE

I died in their arms, throat slit
at the top of the mountain.
Blood rivered my arms, dripped
to earth and the great rock split
to swallow the innocent. Oh,
they dropped me in without time for
the breath of a western reef egret—
swift, not solemn. No one cried
for me, for the beautiful body spent
at their hands. No, they were afraid—
the summer was too dry, the oracle
said—or they thought it said—
sacrifice, but the heat
kept on and I forgot myself in decay—
heat, blackness, a shadow, and then
much later the rains.
                  I sprouted
into tree. I remembered what I used to be.

I remembered.
              They forgot.

II

Want

January 1965

Across the field hay bales make mountains of the snow.
Cattails glisten along the field's bordering ditch
with the crystallization of sun-melted, night-frozen flakes.
Sparrows whir in the castles of glass-coated lilac bushes;
there the wind hushes them to sleep as stars take over the sky.
A coyote calls behind the house. It is the warmth.
It sees through to the night-lighted windows of the child's room.
Its green eyes pierce the heavy white air.
Every night this winter, it returns, calls to the child, waits.
Every morning it will trudge through haunch high snow.

First Year In The District

The call of cicadas
against latch-locked windows
doesn't reach the woman
in the red brick building
across from mine. It reaches me,
and I dream of that house in the country,
Whitewater's constant chatter of crickets
and bullfrogs and wind rustled leaves.
Dream of deer eating tulips on Big Spring Drive,
out the picture window, the chipmunk
packing bird feeder corn into his cheeks.
That meteor shower night
when Gramma and I watched stars fall
across fields, accompanied by cows
who hadn't yet gone home.

16th October 1811

Mr. Hill warns
watches everywhere: St. Pancras
crawling with them. Islington,
Newington, too. Scouts returned
without leads. What about the poor,
Jack asks, Will anyone notice?

Interception

To Her 14-Year-Old Daughter

Under the field lights we cheered
for the game-winning interception,
#13 down low for the tackle sprung
up, curled his arms around the ball and ran;
your father wrapped his arm around me,
slid me closer on the metal stands, his nose
pressed briefly to my hair, rough lips
against my neck—Freshman year of college—
the game ended; I don't remember
the score—I remember his hand sweating
with mine in my flannel lined pocket,
my chest flushing when we reached
the dorm door as he gently shoved me
against the cream brick, hands slipping
up under my coat and I said, *No, not*
now, not like this. A quick peck. I rushed
inside.

A Brace Of Pheasants

In the cold, his shot reverberates:
air and crystals of ice crack from the tree.
They drop as quick as the eyes of the buck.
He expects the world to still to silence.
Instead, a brace of pheasants crash the brush.
A throaty *korr kok* echoes, gnarled branches groan,
and in the man, vessels constrict and blood
rushes, body gut heavy and goose-bumped.
The crumpled mass of the white-tail now
in front of him. He gurgles back a sigh.
Not a young buck. He's done this many years.
Still the mass of soft straw bristles, taut
haunch muscles, bulbous brown eyes, break him
for a moment—silence, all he wants.

In The Anatomy Theater:
Dissection Of Loose Woman

Witness the body's miracle,
curtain of flesh drawn open. See
sternum, fine china-white ribs
like scaffolding encases vital
organs. Count them with me—one,
two, ten true and two floaters. Here
smooth muscle connects, protects.
It is quite elastic, the way it bounces
back against the mallet's even
pressure. Later you will see how
it follows up the back, links along
the spine to stand upright. Cause
of death, anyone? Look closer,
behind the fingerling ribs—
engorgement. No woman has a heart
that large, a prime case of carditis.

See, too, the atrophied arteries,
useless. Limp as stormed worms.
We will skip the stomach for now,
it is of the least interest being best
understood, but what shall I show
next—liver? Lungs? Womb? Ah,
yes, I agree, what wonders of womb
may we find today? Will we be
lucky? I must lengthen the flap as so,
slit abdominal muscles, use the most
controlled incision—we mustn't
harm any specimen. Ah, yes, here
we have gestation, pink curling mass.
Fleshed cord connecting to globular
sack, the very source of life here,
for you, at the mercy of our knives.

23rd October 1811

Jack is unruly. Caught him strangling a beggar. A famous one, at that. No sense in the boy.

John Wilkes Booth's Pocket Diary

Plucked from your pocket, they ruffled
my pages, found answers more than they wanted,

buried me in the whirl of conspiracy.
Tonight I will once more

try the river
with the intent to cross

After days I hold no record of, Stanton studied the script
etched across my dates once more.

though I have a greater desire
and almost a mind

to return to Washington
Never a witness in the trials, my shorn sheets

now under investigation. Great men may fall.
I am silent.

and in a measure
clear my name

Dear John, I know only what I am.
Kidney, liver, lungs missing, I hold nothing but the heart.

Grace On Our Farm, Age 10

Bobby socked, she sits
perched upon the fender
of the black Chevy Coup,

curly hair escaping pigtails.
The car like a shroud behind her,
though there is no death,

no coffin containing the end
of a family that should've
lasted. Instead, beside her

and her transplanted
clench-toothed smile
stands her Uncle Milo, a young

twenty-something, grinning
with a brotherly tilt towards Grace,
her soft hands laid in her lap.

This is the late 40s and there are
rules, roles, expectations
and a grandmother, watching

as if from the 19th century,
dressed in a striped blouse and skirt set,
beneath our willow.

Unrest

In the cemetery of your mind,
the dead don't rest peaceful.

No, they overturn
their own gravestones,
fling dirt from their hair
at you.

The Keeper

I am the nothing
under the nothing
of snow silence
at night. Worm fed
fat by compost, grabbed
and packaged.

I am life's
slow decent
beneath a beehive
tomb, ripped open
by troweling men, pickaxes
in their brains.

I am the brittle moss-
hair plastered
to the faces
of bog-body girls,
fetal forms curled
around the tips of spades.

I am keeper of souls,
caretaker of the pieces
of bodies placed
on display. I am
the everything,
the everyone in one,

the hanging ice,
those wintry fingers
waiting on the doorframe
to brush windblown hair,
to whisper to the lost, waiting
to decay in sun, waiting to lie

down again in the hollows
of that place where the gods
once danced
before we sent them away.

Long Distance

March: Visiting the Week Before

Dirt clouds follow tractors on the feather edges of Indy,
trimming overgrown field boundaries,
cracking the land for the implant.
Black birds cluster in the one old oak,
calling in the spring morning.
There is a fire somewhere near. Wind carries
pine cologne—a memory of Maine's
lush green background in the foreground
of his RAV4: puffy, swollen ankles.
Ri poked his finger into the engorged
flesh, watched as it held the shape,
then refilled. Water retention. The first sign
we tried to ignore.

II

Last July

Genetic. They say. Transplant.
Dialysis? No, not yet. *Yet?*

If it comes to that, he says
later, reporting back, if

it comes to that—
It won't, I say. *It won't.*

III

August Through September

Eight rough red kidney beans line my plate:
This little kidney's too big,
This little kidney has stones,
This little kidney's blood type AB,
This little kidney he won't let get tested at all.

Pinpricks dust arms like freckles,
but freckles are all I have. So I chant
songs of the beans bouncing in the box
before I soak them overnight, I chant
their bubbling whispers in the pan
the next day when they boil, give up
their lives to sustain another.

IV

October Results

Mother:	Negative.
Father:	Negative.
Brother:	Negative.

V

November

Negative.
Negative.
Negative.
Negative.
Negative.
        Let me.
        No.
        You
        don't
        like
        hospitals.

        *

Positive: Evan.
Positive: Jen.

VI

December: Round 2 Testing

Everything shushes—the snow
sheeting out the window, the air
sweeping through the trees.
Don't speak they seem to say,
Shhhhhhh. Don't speak.
The squirrels agree, grasping
slick branches as they seek
shelter. Chichichiiii they say.
Chichichiiii they call to one
another. The time for holding
breaths is here.

VII

January

My apartment hall is shrieking again,
red lights seizuring. Not one door
swings open in the hall.

> The doctors said it was a go,
> your cousin Jen in the final stages,
> last blood test drawn, the results—

In the lobby, firemen speak
with the concierge. They wave
us in from flurried wind. False alarm.

VIII

March: The Week After Visiting

Ri is corpse flat on a table, split open. I know because his mom called. She didn't say it like that, she said, *Evan's kidney is not out yet, but Ri is ready to get it when it happens.* I was up all night, tripping over s-shaped f's for a diplomatic transcription of Dryden's *All for Love* and waiting for a call from Indy at 4 AM so we could say goodbye and I could say *Good luck* before Ri had to leave. On the metro with my visiting cousin, on the way to the Library of Congress, I can't get over the idea of Ri on a table, anesthetized, cracked, with hands in the cavern of his lower stomach. I've seen the shows, the medical dramas where the doctors have lush gelled hair and they talk about their lives while their hands delve inside a patient, and I'm sweating with their talk of superfluous things like vacations and sex lives while their hands twist inside this man, cutting and splicing his body with another.

30th October 1811

Hattie insists I turn him away.
Complicated matter. She does
not know. If he were to talk…
We would all be implicated.

Flutterbies

The words
are coming
reverse in—
stress maybe,
maybe stress—
floating milkweeds
along monarchs,
golden red-orange
wings bright
against a sky
cloudy with shafts
of light—It looks
like a spalien
aceship—marks
of confusion crease
our faces and we
laugh, backwards
working, skies
to the eye.

Trench 2A: Big Spring Drive

I find her in what once was the ditch,
wrapped in a cattail woven sheet,
surrounded by bullfrog carcasses.
A small trauma to the pelvis—
no doubt the result of crashing
a mini bike into a boat trailer hitch
in early adolescence.

In the leathery purse of her stomach:
sesame seeds—she is not native
or they were trading or she'd been gone
for so long,
             so long.
Sacrificed to familial wars,
sibling feuds, who gets what
when the elders die. She
is the silent chronicler of their lives,
watching behind worm eaten eyes.

To The Stag

You ghost my edges, blur
when I turn my head,
dark haunches running
through hunted woods.
In time, I will become
your saltlick, tempt
you to the clearing,
fall for your rough tongue.
It is written, carved
in the trunk of an oak,
wound scabbed
and knotted. Stag,
don't startle at that
other man, don't freeze
in Ri's headlights. Buck
up, head down. Drive
velvet antlers cracking
glass. I'm tired
of waiting for change.

Pomegranate

   Eat from this
palm,   take
the   blood-red
  seeds, watch

 tongue tips touch,
lick and   twirl,
taste   the bitter
   tang. Watch

 the hissing snakes
lisping   over lips,
dripping   down
  to ground. Watch

them congeal
at the end
of the Avenue
of the Dead,
on the steps
of the Pyramid
of the Moon,
watch them sink
below earth
into darkness,
into fire,
watch

the gristled   spray
                of   decapitation
    shimmering   like shark's
teeth,
        ready—

Interception

To Her 23-Year-Old Daughter

Under the field lights we cheered
for the game-winning interception,
#13 down low for the tackle sprung
up, curled his arms around the ball and ran;
a man who was not your father—all blue
eyed with bags of study stamped
below them—wrapped his arm around me
and I slid closer on the metal stands, his nose
pressed briefly to my hair, soft lips against
my neck—Freshman year of college—
the game ended; I don't remember
the score—I remember his hand sweating
with mine in my flannel lined pocket,
my chest flushing when we reached
the dorm door as I roughly shoved him
against the cream brick, hands slipping
up under his coat and I said, *Now,*
right now. Not a quick
peck. I tugged him inside.

The Question

To say yes is to change everything:
the wide open world slipped from my fingertips.
I will become my mother, everything
she fought to keep me from becoming.
The 58-facet round cut diamond glitters, raindrops
lit by lightning, a crystal ball to the past.

Alone she loaded the three of us into her car,
soft soccer cleats draped by the strings over
an arm, delivered us to our games.
Our lone cheerer, planning out the week's
dinners. Hair twisted untidily back. No time
for anything, but for us little monsters, demanding.

Lights dimmed in your basement, dusk
settles over us. Sprawled on the felt flesh
of the pool table, my winning game cut
short by your recklessness. Tongue
tucked behind teeth, wordless, I focus
on the apple red of your bitable lower lip.

If I kiss you, will this go away?
As lips crash and swell, flooding
the animals beneath the heart
will we become blood craving beasts,
briefly forgetting we ever existed,
resetting time to before this moment?

III

Seduce Me Outside

There are many ways snow can kill:
of course hypothermia,
avalanche, building collapse,
                              the car
quick-biting off unplowed roads.
Then the ways we never think of
until we're in the center of coyote
band, their too-human
                              teeth glistening
as they tap claws in unison
against the snow's iced cap,
and carol.
            Or the white owl which nips
flesh from exposed faces, gnaws
into the muscle unwrapping the pale
cheekbone once busted by a brick.
The robins endangered
                              by April
blizzard and the cherry blossoms iced.
What I mean: an avalanche
does not kill much
                              quicker, my fingers
bandaged in gloves and always the wet
falling snow, out a northern window,
mimics elegance deadly. Again.
                              Again.

Demeter

Gods don't age, and yet she feels
her body—a twenty-five year-old body

break in weariness. No one
believes in her, no one leaves

bunches of golden grains
to feed her and her favor.

Her only child has fallen
into bliss with her husband

and their dark-haired, black-eyed
children who she isn't allowed

to visit. What's the point?
She asks of no one, letting down

the curls coiled around her skull.
Last year droughts and droughts

burning up the corn, cracking
the foul earth looking for a way in.

No such luck. Just starvation
and wildfire and death.

This year she brandishes her grip
on winter, letting April snow.

They call this climate change,
she laughs, *oh don't they know*.

The Hive In Winter

Up close, a humming. Constant
shimmer of wings for warmth.
All winter, they mass and vibrate,
proboscises tonguing reserves
of honey. This is the most
dangerous time for the hive. Already
the surrounding snow is littered
with carcasses. Survival is
in numbers. This hive he's named
Clara, after his granddaughter.
Who will tell her, if they die?

1st November 1811

Dogs flew at us. Watches increased
last week. To Islington. 1 small.
Too long in ground. Retreated
after hasty re-covering. Jack desperate.

Oracle

There is nothing I can do.
My expertise is in the dead,
Grampa, and you are not
just yet. I stare at the white
wall of my apartment.
Try excavating mind-fields.
Sift for something particular,
a memory to hold
onto instead of the ache.

The last time they told me you were dying—
organs failing, skin translucent as onion flesh—
you soared back.

I will beat the ground
until earth cracks,
spits out the prophecy
I want to hear—   instead
my fists produce
the faintest whisper.
I barely catch it as the oracle takes flight, harnessing the breeze—
        He'll die in   their   arms

After The Hospital Waiting Room

It's times like these we don't eat.
Not that we've forgotten to, but
more like our body forgot its need.
In times like these, the body
is occupied by other hungers,
the emptiness not from not eating,
from the potential of loss, of death.
The body wants to fill itself,
so at night, after leaving the hospital's
burning antiseptic scent,
I drag my empty body to your house, Stag,
and let you fuck me quickly, repeatedly,
filling me with your need for me,
the void between my heart and stomach
briefly satisfied. Your clean laundry
and pine odor sticks to me,
disguising the scent of another death
I'll never be ready for.

The Damned

Forgive us
our trespasses
in want
of bread.

5th November 1811

My Hattie gone. Child sickly. 1 large
at Newington. £6 from Mr. Rhine.

When Asked About My Grandfather's Death

It was sudden and not so sudden
as when after some time and none at all
you reach mutual climax, thinking
it would never happen but knowing
with the rhythm of this man
you've known before, like you
know death—knowing both in the end
would come.

The Body Wants

But if that's what the body wants, to be
dead and buried—worm-meal and fertilizer—who am I
to argue? His body quit. His mind was there until the end or
until the morphine kicked in, anyways. His mind
knew what the body wanted and wanted it in that resigned
yet fearful way,
                    the way my mind wants what my body craves
—you—but my mind doesn't care for the pain
of wanting but not having you and so, fearful
that this *kindred spirit* fucking will likely end
up hurting us all—you, your girl, Ri, and me—but
not more than not giving in now, the mind resigns
itself to the body, to the way you feel against me—
a little like death, every time.

Walking Milwaukee After A Death

The movie projector clattered
into view, clattered the morning
open, dull blue and fog,
clattered cardinals awake and the cat-
bird caterwauling from some ledge.
The picture was unclear—azul,
hazed, continuously rolling the same
shot, the film blue-burned
by unexpected light. And it flickered
well like all good old movies
should. And it flickered blue grains
against a cream brick building and it
flickered, shimmered, spewed—no
movie, just a busted fire hydrant on Canal,
on a cold, cold day in June.

Expiration

I am afraid to love you, Ri, certainly,
that is part of it. Watching Grampa die
these last seven years, watching
his body shrink as the heart struggled
to pump, listening for the phone
at 1 AM, finally turning it off
in the terror of not knowing when
it would happen. As it happened,
it wasn't a pre-dawn call
like the first time, 3 AM, and mother's
voice—*Get up. Your Grandpa's dying.*
Midday. The sun bolted bright in the sky.
False alarm. A week later the real call.
A voicemail. Early evening.
And you weren't here. I cannot forgive
that. My family at his bedside when he passed.
And me, alone, in DC. The same
as when you went into surgery
two years ago for a kidney transplant.
The sun also shining that day, I sweated
through the thin linen of my shirt
in the unusual March heat wave, knowing
that you were dying faster than me—still are.

The Undertaker To His Apprentice

It is better not to witness
the phrenologist's visit, better

to accept the coins, slink
into some secluded corner,
unable to say for sure

whether anything happened,
or is missing. Better, too,

not to check the coffin
after. I made the mistake
once. Saw the sawed nub

where the head no longer
sat. The flesh severed

uncleanly for haste's sake,
tendon ribbons ripped,
so white against the blood.

Vertebrae twisted near
90 degrees. I've seen bodies

hacked, bowels streaming
from sliced stomachs, but
nothing compares to the headless.

Seal the coffin as soon as
the phrenologist leaves and keep

coffin nails in constant
supply. Cover my coffin
with heavy stones when I die.

Unease

It is unsettling, how earth slowly sunk on the grave post-rain.
They'll fill it, you say, meaning the depression over his body—
casket, his casket. We wandered half an hour trying to remember
where we buried him that day in June, found a hen-specked bird
refusing to startle above his head. Or feet. Oak branches hang
heavy in July heat, leaves crinkled beyond repair. Grass crunches
beneath my shifting. Drought. The cool air had turned shortly after
we had tucked the spring morning and twenty-one white carnations
into his waterproof vault (he never learned to swim). The lake edge
recedes daily from the cemetery. Soon, we'll be able to stand in it.

7th November 1811

On watch at St. Thomas's. Indecent
proposal from Jack. He will come.
I know what he will say. £8.30s.

After Rain

It is not the first time
I've sunk into mud
let it swallow my feet,
inhale my legs to the bony
knees. It is not
the first time I've dreamt
of burying myself, feeding
my body to the worms and beetles,
sticking around in just
enough pieces to warrant
archaeological investigation.
I'll excavate myself,
metatarsals to pelvis,
pelvis to sternum, sternum
to vertebra C 1—there is no
skull—carried off by some
animal—except for fragments
of the jaw, enough to whisper—
take me from this place, piece
me back together, put me on
display—

Ribs 3 through 7 exhibit
spiny nodules,
those would've formed a cage
around the heart, and what
about those hands,
boy hands.
Not thin and slender
but sturdy—I wire
each carpal together. They feel
each other, tentatively
at first, checking
every member, and satisfied,
leap free. Twirl before me. Dance.

Autumn Walk With Stag

All the leaves softly whisper,
calling with the owl tall in the trees.
Listen—*all of us*—ominous
voices lapping our long faces.—
you can trust, all of us—Rustling
along the street an omnibus. As from
a dream, a doll drives,
bus wheels bright red balls
and the stoplight quickens its flashing
then falls down crashing two steps
from where we are. It melts into the ground,
lost. Found a hundred thousand
years later by troweling anthropologists
(they've taken the roles of archaeologists).
A small mouse grovels for a scrap
of anything, the air heavy with a foul
density of rot—only you realize
that is not now. The smell of warmly
rotting leaves, musky like your lover,
brings you back.
          Love, I'm right
here. It's fall. Forget this night upon us.

Back To The Source

Amongst Gramma's knick knacks lining
the built-in shelf—built by his own hands—
in the dining room which was once the whole
house, the carcass of a hummingbird, luminescent
lime feathers still attached, preserved, naturally,
from decay. My grandpa, keeper of dead things.

Years later and he's dead as that hummingbird,
as absent, too—his chair filled by one of the cats
waiting to be plucked up and into his lap—one
of the cats who probably ran off with the hummingbird.

In its place, a red throated woodpecker picked up only
a few months before for reasons we'll never be able to
say, or ask, but know are beyond blood and bone.

Snow Holds

Because I am visiting home,
I shovel snow
pregnant with more
than the average moisture
as it whites out the world,
houses merely mountains,
houses the peaks of Swiss Alps
where lies a castle carved
from so much ice—a glacier
like my grandparents' fountain,
dug by Grampa and his brothers
in their well-digging days
and stacked with stones that moss
and ice cling to easily. Once,
when the snow-globing stopped,
roads barely drivable,

there we were, Maria and I
in snowsuit onesies
building an igloo along the side
of the house on Big Spring Drive
and warming our faces
against the fluffed air
from the dryer vent.
Grampa came outside packed
in a puffy coat to get the mail,
the tip of his fingers glowing,
sending smoke signals.
It was the first time we caught him.
We spoke in whispers.
Invisible in snow. The vent
melting the floor of our fort.
It is warm now, too.

Ivory

Here, I am stranger—ochre sand
slung against bones, staining
sidewalks, socks. Even brick
buildings are redder from bloodied
wind. I am afraid to stand still,
to absorb raw umber, burnt
sienna, to become unrecognizable
to you. These bones are porous—
Dad always worried I wasn't
drinking enough milk. Sometimes
I feel like driftwood, rainbow trout
living in the crevices without
my welcome, and I am, but
on land and the trout are
assorted beetles and red worms,
a few ecru grubs. They all want.
Even you, my Stag. Your twelve
points de-fleshed me, left me
to bleach in Rock Creek Park,
nurturing the city as the city
became me. The bones hum,
riddled with your imprints.
Isn't this what you wanted?
What you always wanted, rubbing
the late fall velvet from your rack?

Consumption

A shot at dawn.
Haunches drenched
with adrenaline
race until the blood
is no longer left
to pump.

Rose petals brace
snow, strewn
trail to lovers' dens.

Follow the rose
petals, feel the warmth
leave the body of a doe.
Split her center—hundreds

of flowers spill forth
and flutter out, taking
to the sky. That night,

we'll devour
her heart.

Passing Time

Grey bearded men joke and smoke, mock-brawling
       on the porch.
The big one, laughing, shakes—ashes shimmer
       falling on the porch.

Ice clinks in lemonade glasses, perspiring spring.
       A honey bee nearby.
Granmma pours refills. The cat curls up. We sit recalling
       on the porch.

He's forgotten her face, tries to recall what's beyond
       the soft curls,
the girl he should've married, while his child is crawling
       on the porch.

When they're all gone, a large rat guards the front door,
       but today kitty
is home. They return to flying fur, watch kitty
       rat-mauling on the porch.

He stands glass-eyed at the door, speaking, though
        she can't make out
words, only her head-cocked reflection and a child's
        bawling on the porch.

My brothers and I are gathered around the iron lace
        table, playing poker.
The youngest throws down his chocolate chips. He's
        all in, on the porch.

Silence, silence answer the phone. You've been waiting.
        Outside, autumn
drops leaves wordlessly. Sit deafly—he'll keep
        calling—on the porch.

Monarch Butterfly

Danaus plexippus (Linnaeus)
has several broods in WI
beginning with mid-May
arrivals. They are documented

throughout the state, tagged
wherever milkweeds are prevalent,
often along woodland edges.
Early broods (May/June/July),

the non-migrants, live 30-40 days.
Late summer fliers, 8-10 months.
These, characterized by smaller
wingspans than their counterparts,

migrate to the tall hills and spruce
forests of Angangueo, Mexico
along gene-controlled circadian
tracks—in WI most commonly

beginning their journey along
Lake Michigan or the Wisconsin
and Mississippi Rivers. It is rare
to see roosts or migrating flocks

inland, shocking even. Mom, Dad,
and I stood—for minutes? hours?—
one August afternoon as an orange
storm raged overhead, engulfed

our maples in flittering flames.
Trapped, nobody ran for the camera.
We stood, moment to moment,
until the last of the flock slipped

from the trees. Our eyes caught
and for another breath, we didn't
need words to understand each other—
remarkable. Even more remarkable,

some of these migrants survive—
the trip to Mexico (pesticides,
cars), the winter—and return,
pale and tattered, home.

The House On Cold Spring Road

Go straight on Cold Spring, past the park where once
the splintering of bone broke the sounds of

our play—ulna, radius teepeed so
casually, it haunted me for weeks. Don't

stop for movies, the Blockbuster's gone and
the grocery store moved across the street, that

strip darkly vacant. The library, too,
has moved and Mrs. Reiman with her clown

costume. She always let us help sort, gave
us treasures, antiques—an aged lace wedding

dress for Barbie, a gold, ruby gemmed brooch,
the pearl accented watch, forever still,

tucked in my jewelry drawer with old coins.
There, on the left, with the red maple, leaves

dense on the front lawn—that's it. Pull in. Stay
awhile. This is where my story begins.

Three Endings

Light lashes the tops of cemetery tree leaves
    and below, this nonsense of nothing
(—hills, we'll remember it as hills when we visit again—)
tripping us up in grief. There a hole. Dug deep. Prepped
    with steel bars—

Thunder-clashes. When he was dying, slices of lightning hung
    like lemon on a full glass of water. A wolf pack packed around
his hospice bed. Their howls rivaling the storm and then the soul
    slipped out on a breath. Grey skies breaking
                to blue, a seam of sunlight.

This is not about death—Roller rink. Fort Atkinson. Ca. 1954.
Grace in a pink skirt. In the corner of the scene: this man. She thinks
he works there. Slip, tumble. See the button skating across the waxed
wood floor. Her eyes: *Could you find me a safety pin?*   His—*Yes.*

A Butterfield Horse

*Sculptor Debra Butterfield builds horses out of driftwood, photographs
them, takes them apart to cast the wood in bronze and reassembles them for
the final sculpture.*

Tangle of branches fished
from waters' edges, bleached
by drift and sun,
                tumbled
        together into horse.

The neck, ungodly long, bows,
                jaw open-mouthed.
      Teeth clip at my shirt
collar,   fling me
upon her back.
          I slip
over a hip and slide inside
        a hollow in her stomach.

Hands curl
          into hooves
                and my stretching neck aches
within this shrinking
space and I
want out.

Wood becomes bronze
in her un-
                building and
          I take
my chance,
                leaping
through her throat
back to solid earth.

She is rebuilt
and I am reborn,
standing back, looking up,
seeing everything
as if for the first time.

NOTES

The italicized lines from JOHN WILKES BOOTH'S POCKET DIARY are quotes from the date book he carried with him and used as a diary after President Lincoln's assassination. It is currently on display in the museum at **Ford's Theatre National Historic Site.**

Acknowledgments

I would like to thank following publications in which versions of these poems first found homes:

Another Chicago Magazine, "After the Hospital Waiting Room"
and "When Asked about My Grandfather's Death"

Atticus Review, "The Hive in Winter"

Bayou Magazine, "Unease"

Cobalt Review, "The Keeper"

Fairy Tale Review, "Ivory"

Hawai'i Pacific Review, "Snow Holds"

Linden Avenue Literary Journal, "The Body Wants"
and "Expiration"

Louisiana Literature, "A Butterfield Horse"

Product, "The Archaeologist in Childhood"

Sou'wester, "The House on Big Spring Drive" and "Want"

TAB: The Journal of Poetry & Poetics, "Keeping On"

The Bleeding Lion, "Consumption"

Zone 3, "Curveball, 1963"

My thanks to the friends, colleagues, and mentors who helped make this book a reality, especially those at American University where most of this collection came into being. In particular, I would like to thank fellow poets Keigh-Cee Bell, Maegan Ramirez, and Sarah Sansolo, whose excellent feedback continues to help me grow as a writer. To my early mentors, Kyle Dargan and David Keplinger, thank you for your guidance and encouragement. Without your support and love of the craft, it would have taken me a lot longer to fall into poetry; I am forever grateful. I must also thank my professors and cohort at the UNIVERSITY OF SOUTHERN MISSISSIPPI'S CENTER FOR WRITERS. And to my publisher, Kurt Lovelace, thank you for finding and believing in my work.

To my family—none of this would have been possible without you. Thank you, mom, for always telling me to go for it, and dad, for supporting me no matter what. To Gramma, whose love of storytelling and reading rubbed off on me. To my brothers, you weirdos. Thank you. And of course, for my grandparents who are no longer with us. I carry your stories in my bones.

Anastasia Stelse
November 25, 2024

Anastasia Stelse

Anastasia Stelse returned to Wisconsin after nearly a decade living in the South, a landscape which continues to paint her writing. She holds a BA in Archaeology and Writing from the University of Evansville; an MFA from American University; and a PhD in English, Creative Writing Emphasis from the University of Southern Mississippi's Center for Writers.

Primarily a poet, she began as a fiction writer and believes in the importance of multi-genre study and practice as vital components of a writer's education.

Her poetry, fiction, and interviews appear in *Poet Lore*, *Sou'wester*, *Crab Orchard Review*, *Narrative*, and the *Memorious Blog*, and other journals. Stelse teaches Business Communication in the Wisconsin School of Business at the University of Wisconsin-Madison.

In addition to writing and teaching, she pursues creative arts including pottery and sewing.

www.ingramcontent.com/pod-product-compliance
Lightning Source LLC
Chambersburg PA
CBHW020423150626
46554CB00014B/2472